ℒove Is...

Discovering
the Beauty
of God's Love
Through
the Heart
of a Child

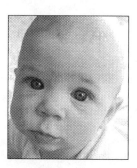

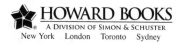
HOWARD BOOKS
A DIVISION OF SIMON & SCHUSTER
New York   London   Toronto   Sydney

O ur purpose at H oward B ooks is to:
- Increase faith in the hearts of growing Christians
- Inspire holiness in the lives of believers
- Instill hope in the hearts of struggling people everywhere
  Because He's coming again!

Published by Howard Books, a division of Simon & Schuster, Inc.
1230 Avenue of the Americas, New York, NY 10020
HOWARD   www.howardpublishing.com
BOOKS

Love Is . . . Discovering the Beauty of God's Love Through the Heart of a Child

ISBN-13: 978-1-4516-4149-3

10 9 8 7 6 5 4 3 2 1

For information regarding special discounts for bulk purchases, please contact: Simon & Schuster Special Sales at 1-800-456-6798 or business@simonandschuster.com.

Project developed by Bordon Books, Tulsa, Oklahoma
Project writing by Shanna Gregor, La Donna Flagg, Rayné Bordon, Jennith Moncrief, and Rebecca Currington in association with Bordon Books
Edited by Chrys Howard
Cover design by Lori Jackson, LJ Design
Cover photo by Greg Jackson
Photo page 23 by L R Legwin/Hulton Archive/Getty Images

All scripture quotations, unless otherwise indicated, are taken from the HOLY BIBLE, NEW INTERNATIONAL VERSION ˚ (NIV ˚). Copyright © 1973, 1978, 1984 by International Bible Society. Used by permission of Zondervan Publishing House. All rights reserved.

Introduction

Who knows the pure joy of loving and being loved with
reckless abandon better than a child? As you flip through the
pages of this book, enjoy these delightful photos that capture
children doing what they do best—just being themselves, fully
confident that they'll be loved for it.

As you read through the captions that accompany these
heart-tugging photos, allow them to draw you into the warm
embrace of God's amazing love. Some of these captions may
be familiar to you since they are based on scriptures. Our
hope as you read through them all is that you will experience
with childlike innocence the immeasurable love God has
for you and that you'll be compelled to share that love with
everyone around you.

If you have heart-tugging pictures of your child, please refer
to the last page to see how you can submit them for future
publication.

There are *moments* in life when everything seems *perfect*.

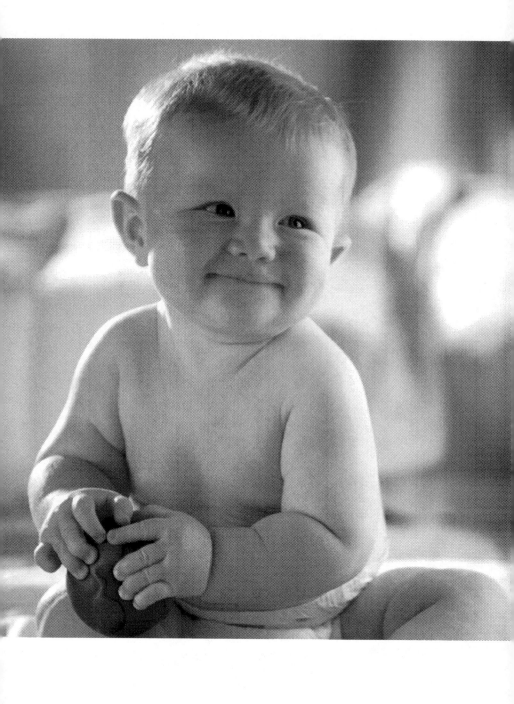

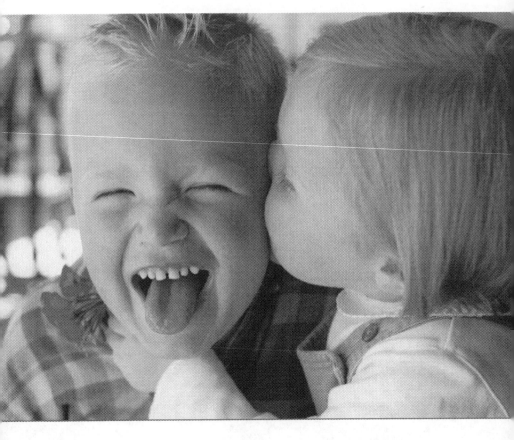

Those moments have to do with *loving* . . .

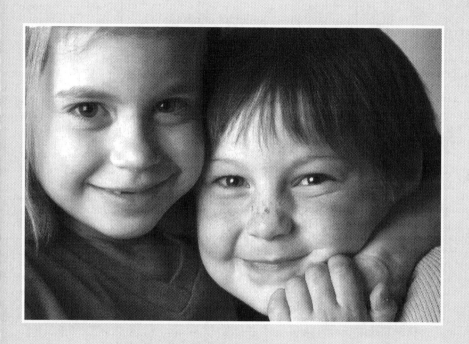

. . . and showing our love for *each other*.

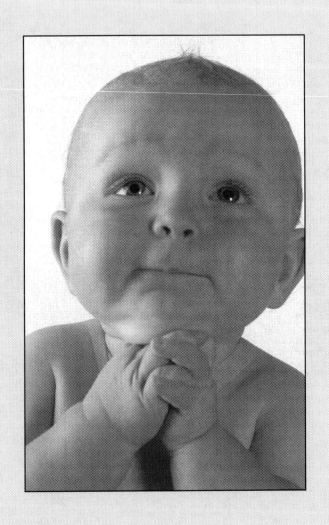

Love is something so much *greater*
than we are.

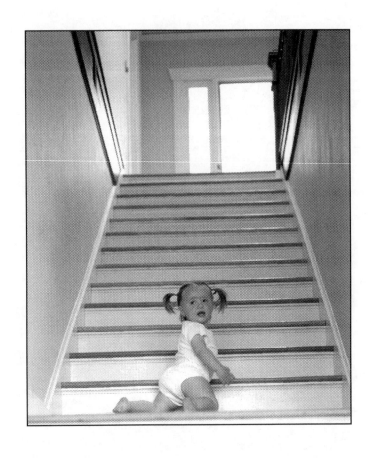

Love believes that it can do *all* things.

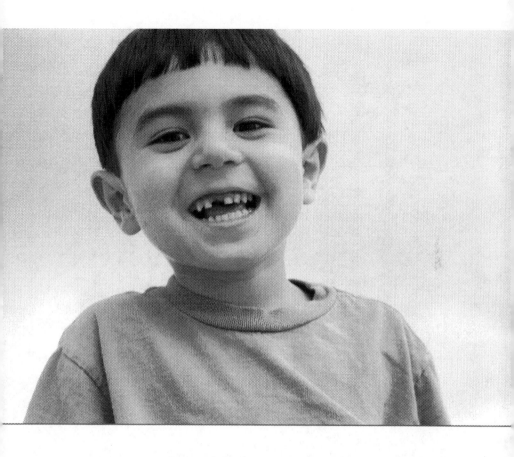

It can fill in the holes
created by your shortcomings.

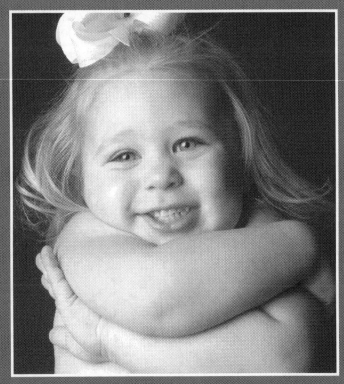

Love helps you embrace
yourself as God created you . . .

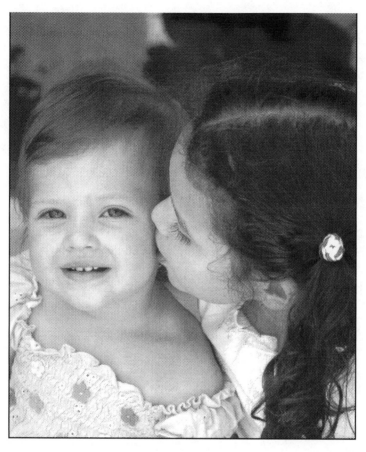

. . . and helps you appreciate others, too.

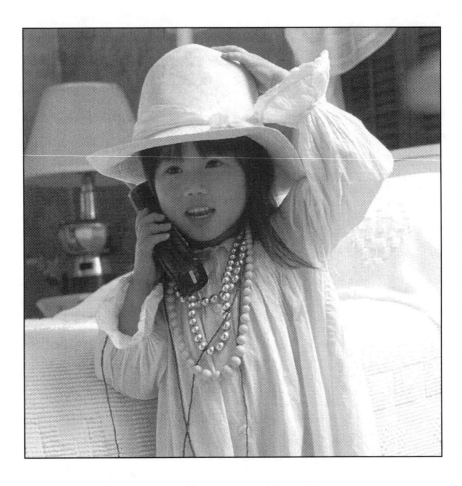

Love gives you a heart makeover . . .

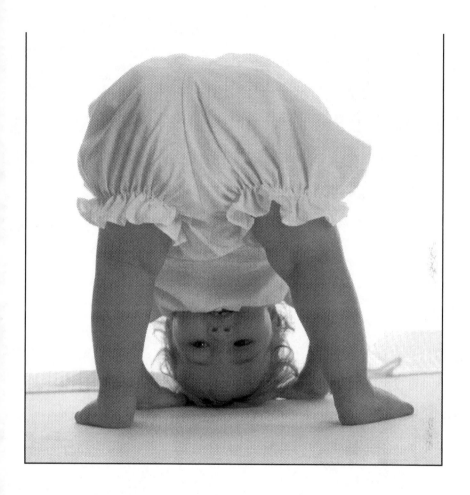

. . . and allows you to be yourself.

Love is patient.

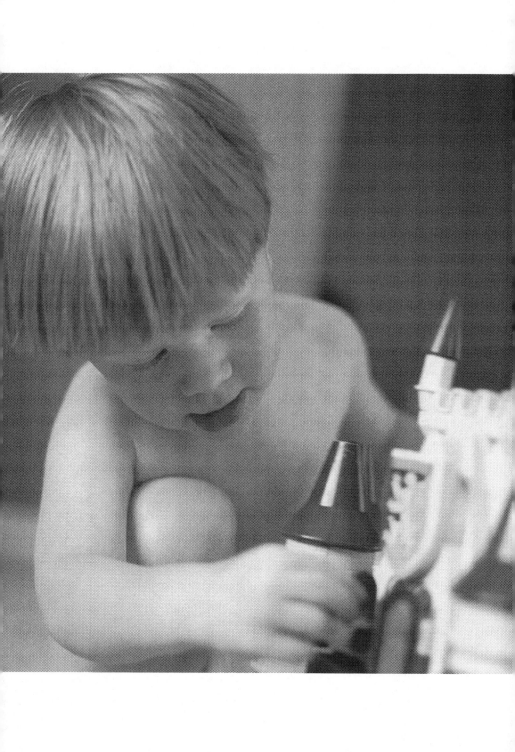

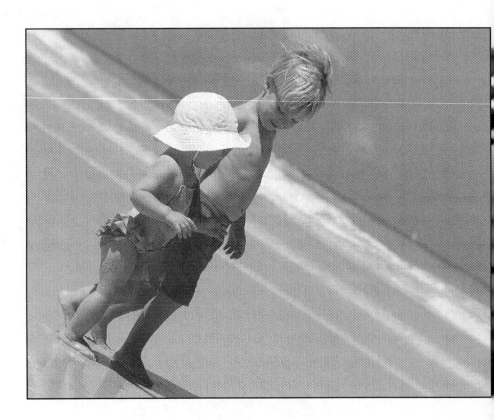

Love is kind.

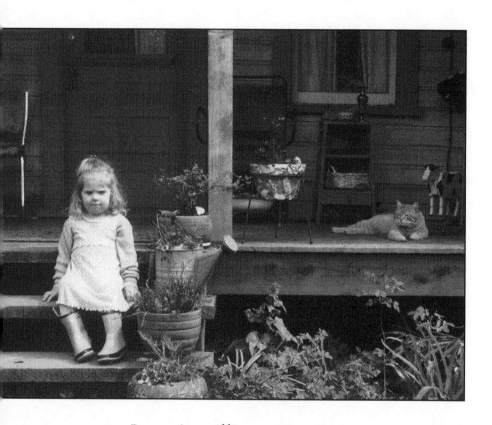

Love is willing to wait.

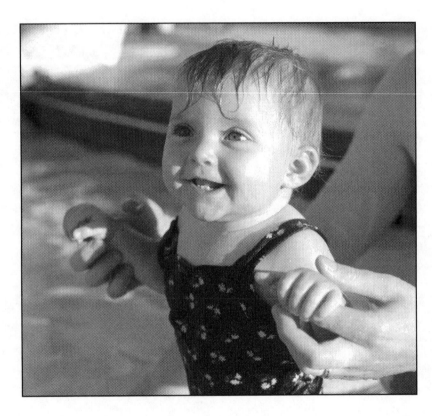

Love trusts.

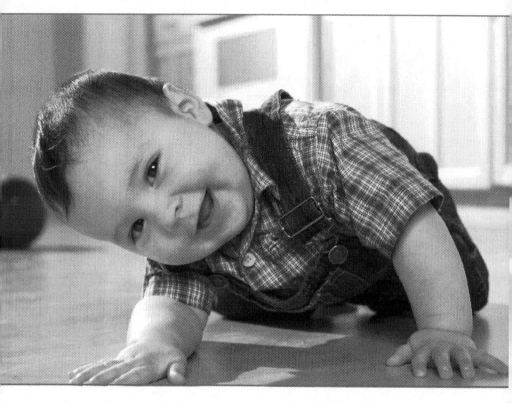

It is a *glimpse* of the *eternal*.

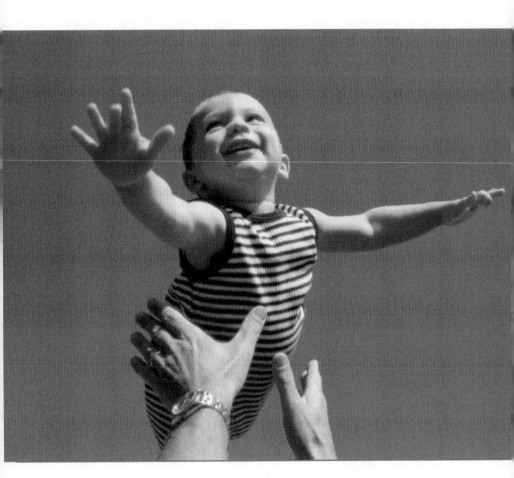

Love knows no bounds.

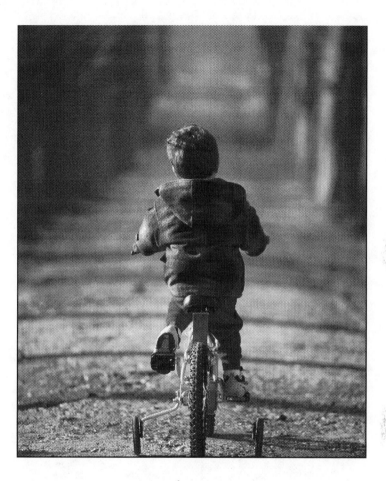

It takes you
where you didn't know
you *could* go.

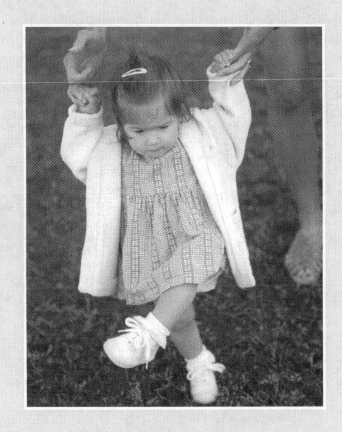

Love *encourages.*

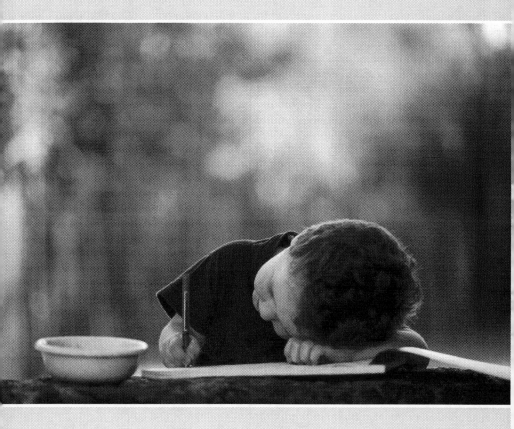

Love *inspires*.

Love can even be unexpected.

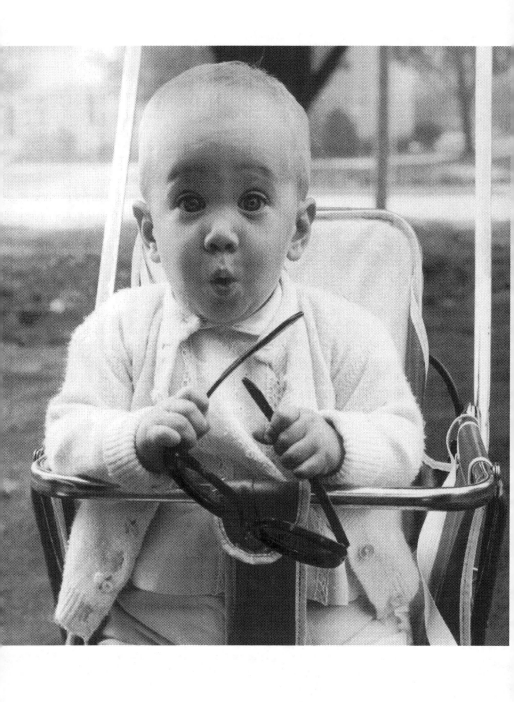

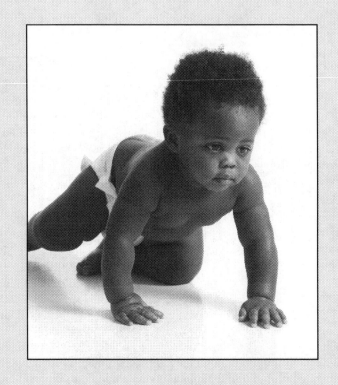

Love *perseveres*.

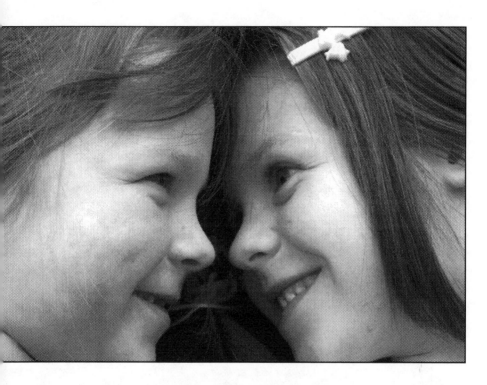

Love is the only force
that can make a potential *enemy* a *friend*.

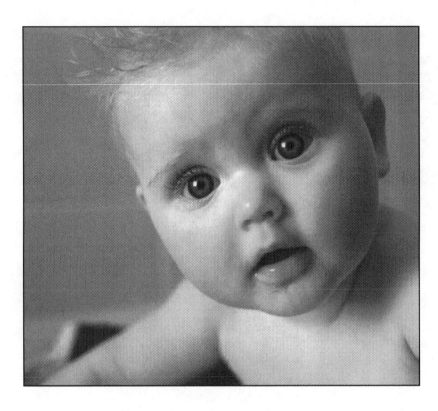

Love opens your eyes.

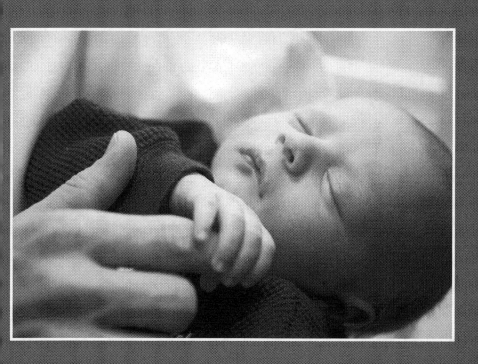

Love never fails.

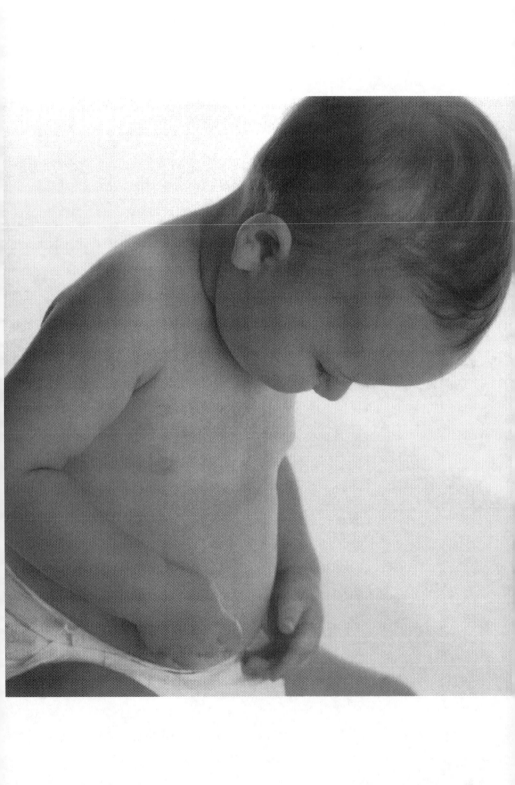

But *where* can you find such love?

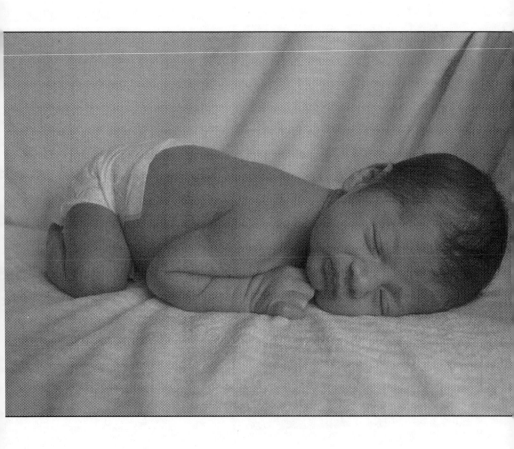

30

God says, "I have loved you
with an *everlasting* love."

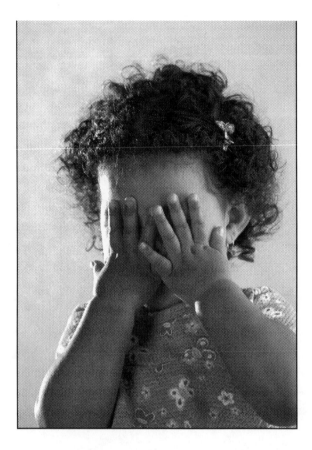

You can't count God's love on your fingers . . .

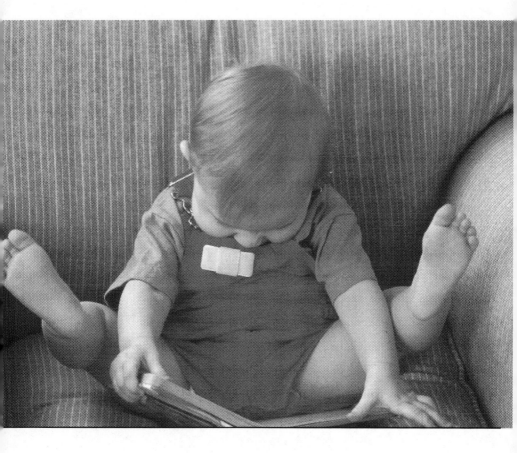

. . . or toes.

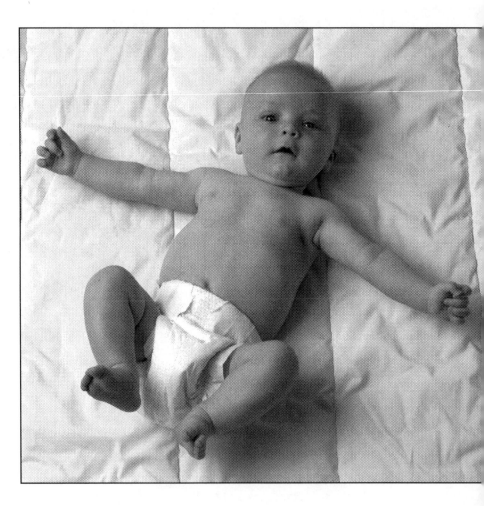

You can only measure it with
the *depth* of your *heart.*

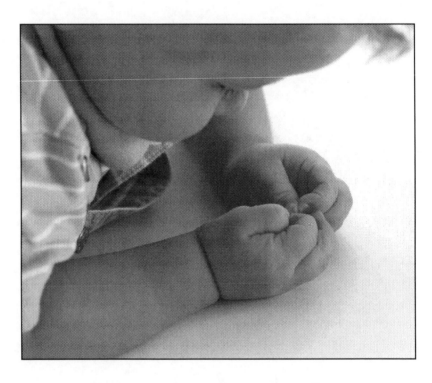

God knows you *intimately* and
loves you completely.

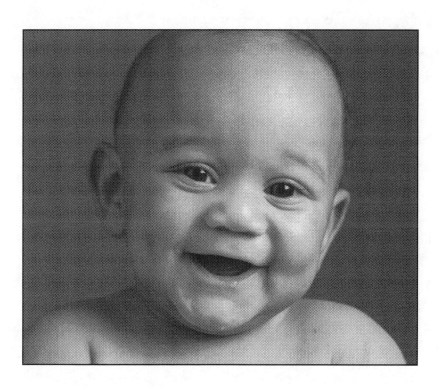

He *smiles* when He thinks of you.

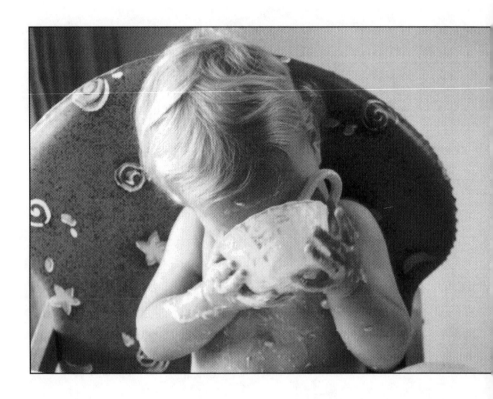

You can be a *mess*;

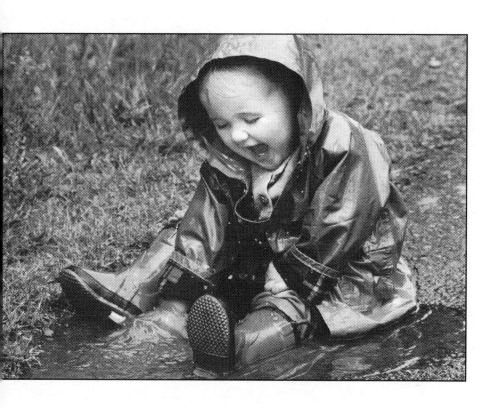

you can be all *wet*;

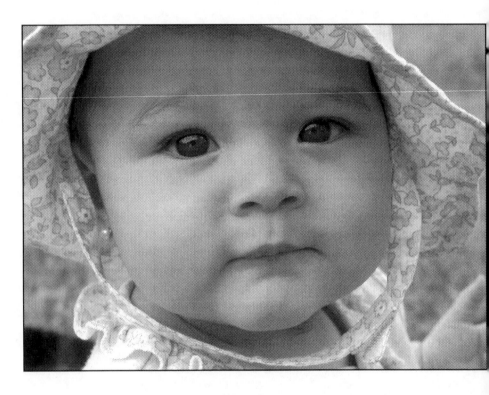

you can be *cute* as a button;

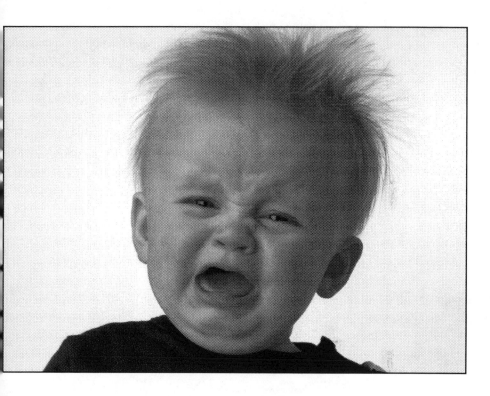

you can be *mad* . . .

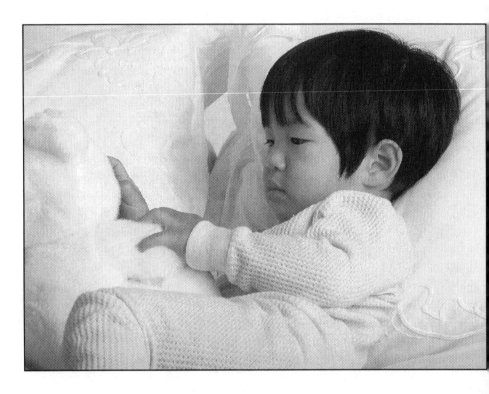

. . . or *sad . . .*

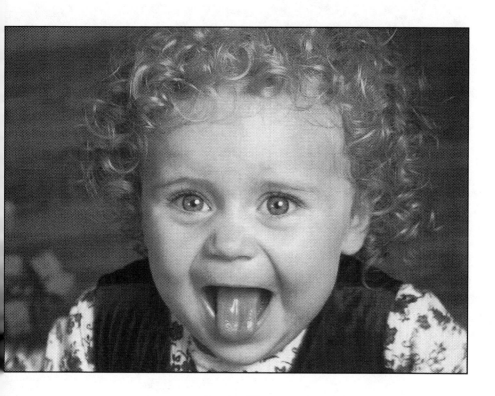

. . . or *silly* . . .

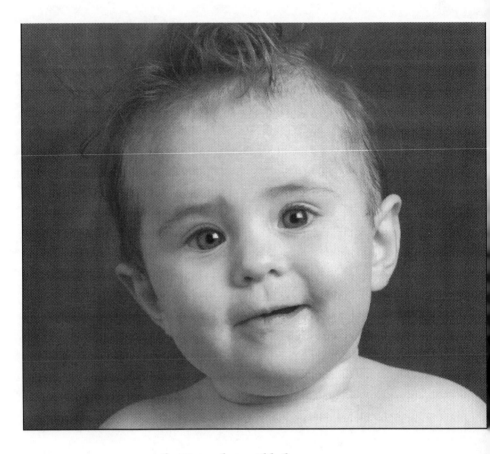

. . . and God still loves you . . .

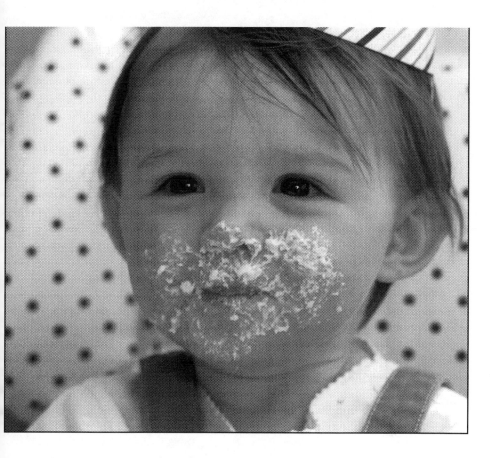

. . . just as you are!

Sometimes *He* is
the only one
who can *comfort* you.

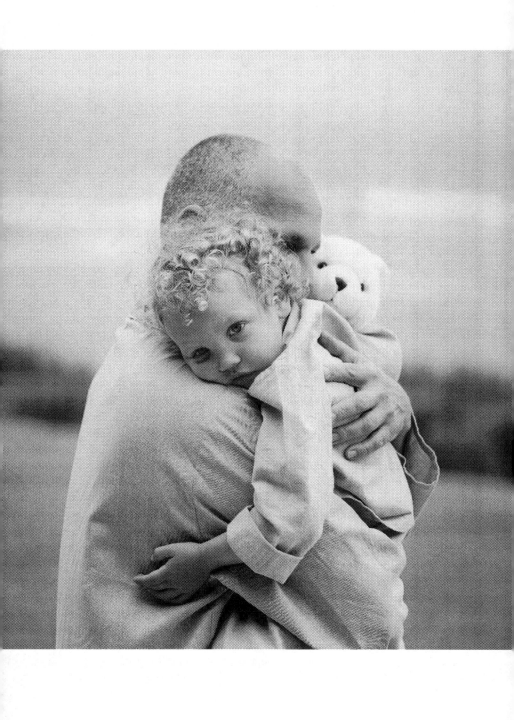

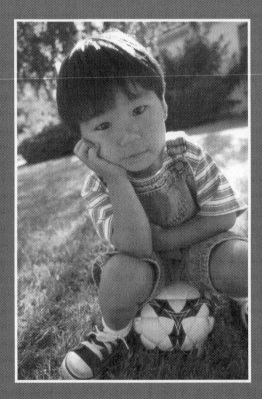

God believes in you
even when you are disappointed in yourself.

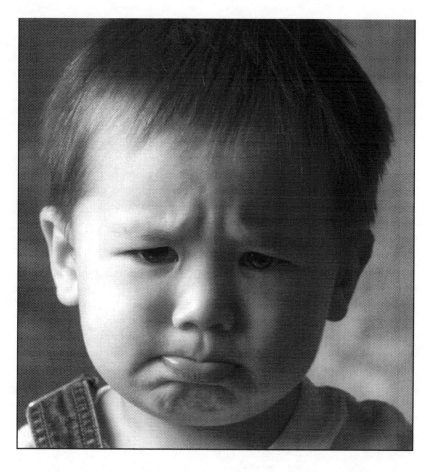

Like the sun rests behind the clouds,
so God's love is present even on difficult days.

He saves all of your tears in His bottle.

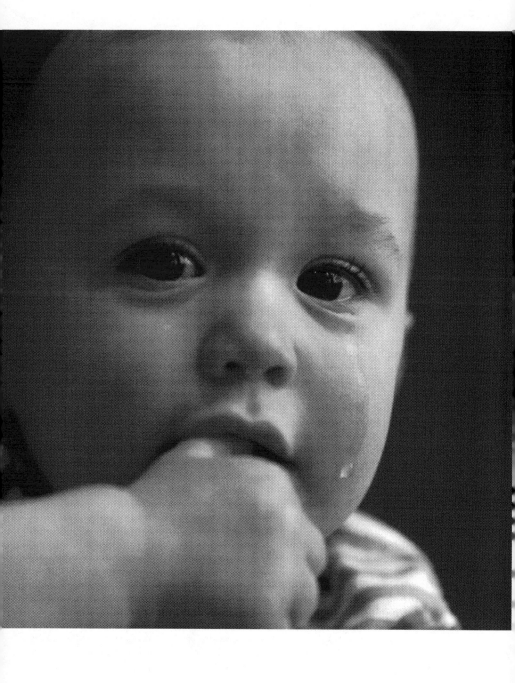

God's love *gives* and *gives* and *gives*.

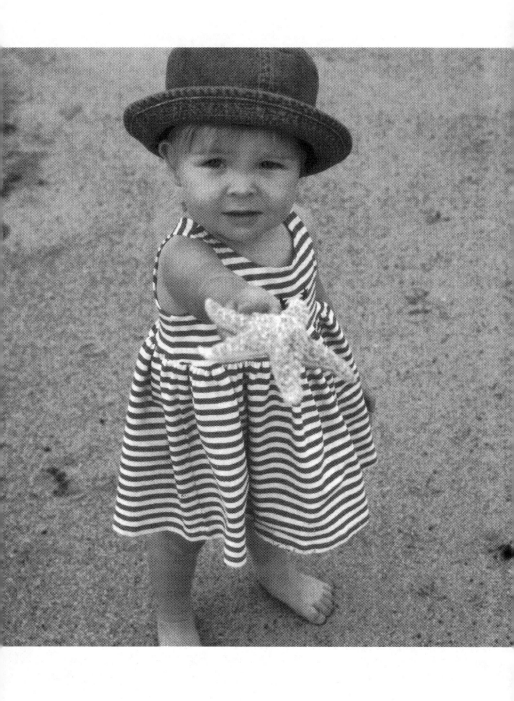

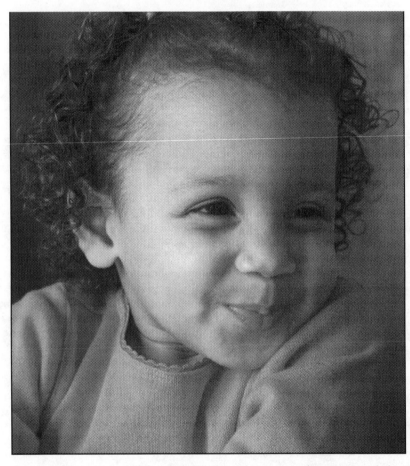

It makes you feel like your weight in gold.

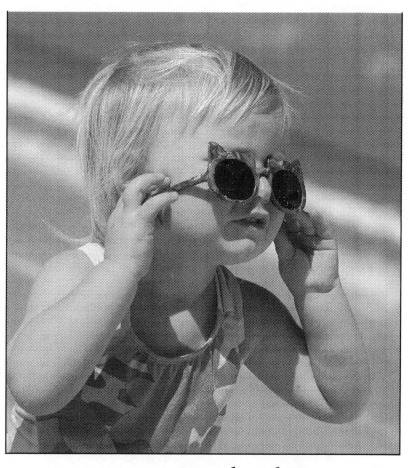

His love shines *brighter*
than all your darkest times.

Where His love reigns,
the very *joy* of *Heaven* itself is felt.

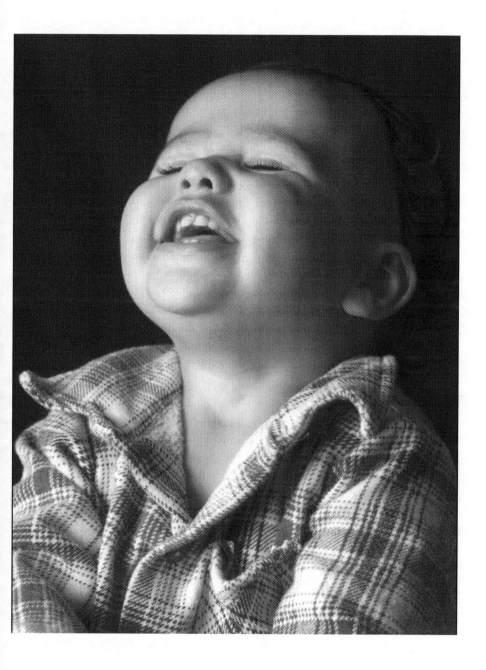

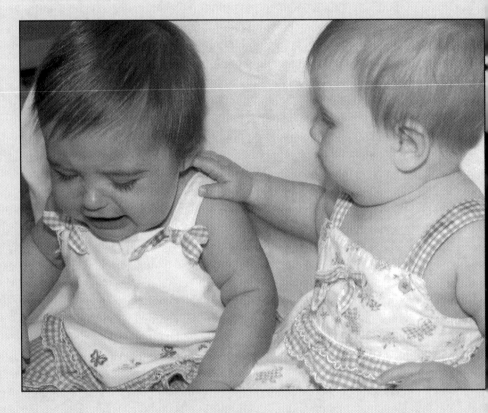

And when you let *Him* love you,
you can pass it on.

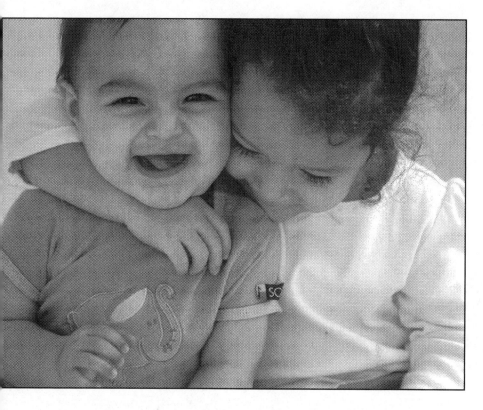

For the Bible says,
"We love because He first loved us."

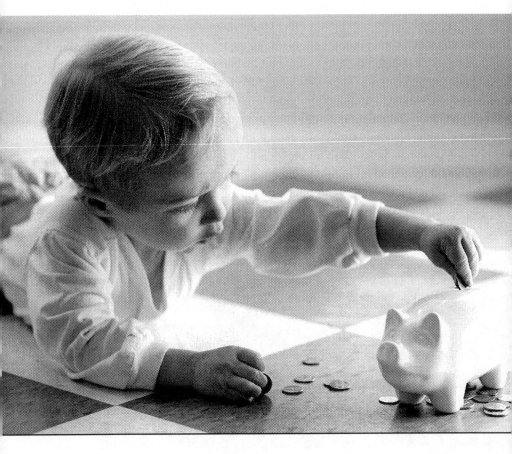

Love is the one business in which it pays to be an
absolute *spendthrift*. So . . .

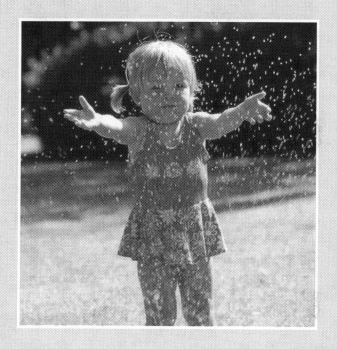

Give it away;

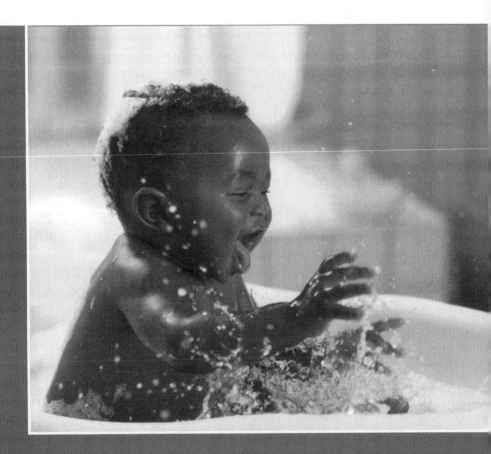

Splash it everywhere;

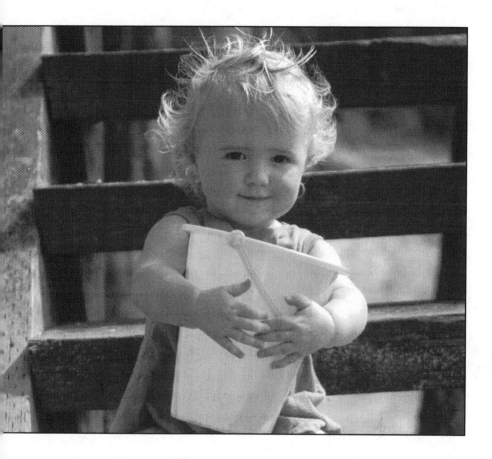

Pour it out;

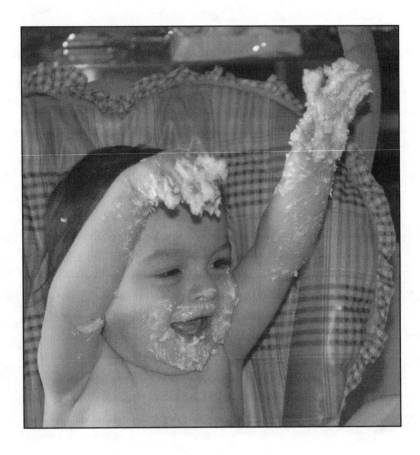

Spread it around;

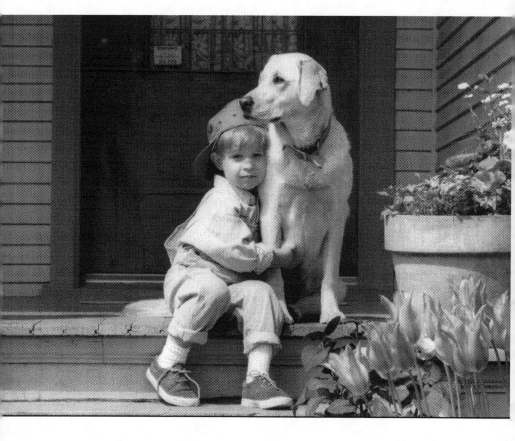

You just can't out give love.

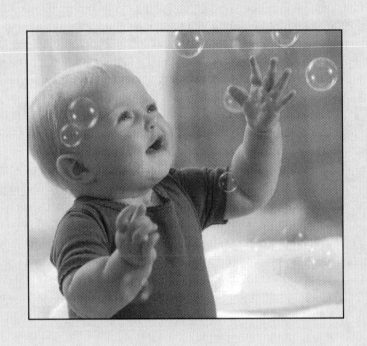

It always comes back to you!

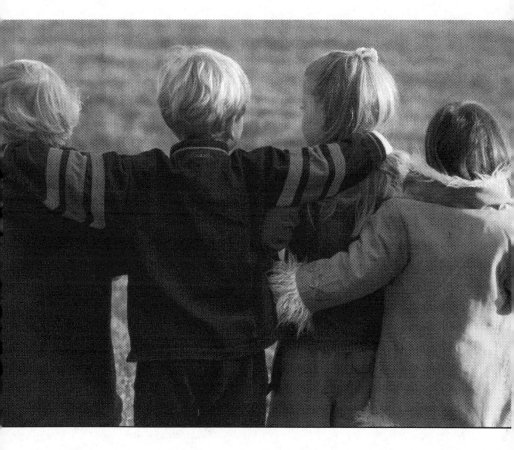

And tomorrow
you'll have *more
love* than ever.

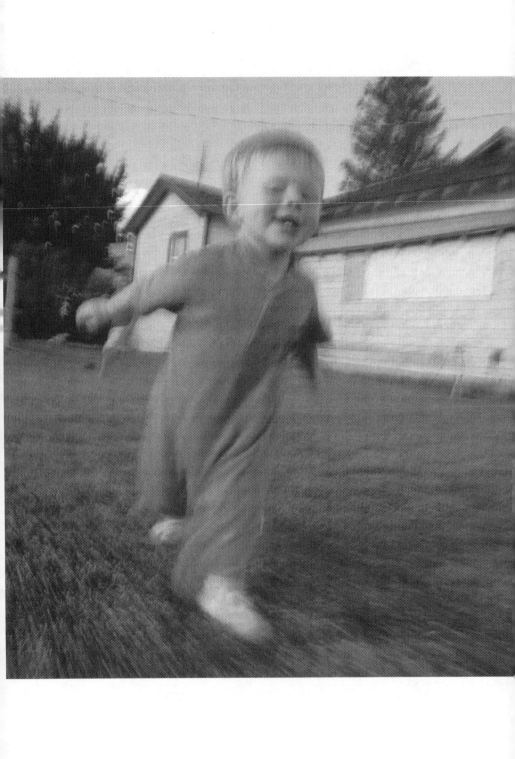

So love with abandon,

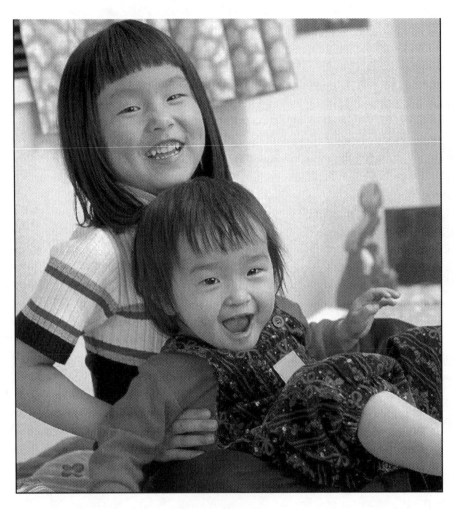

fervently,

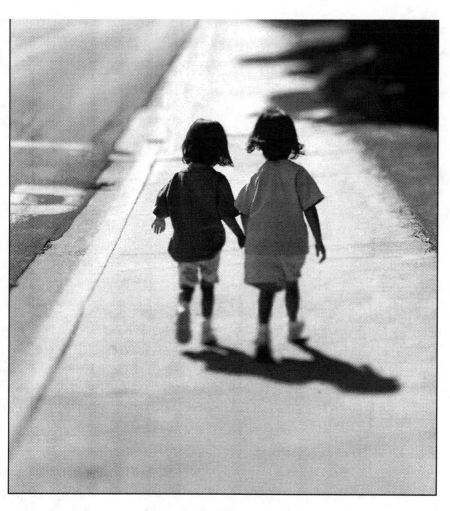

from the heart . . .

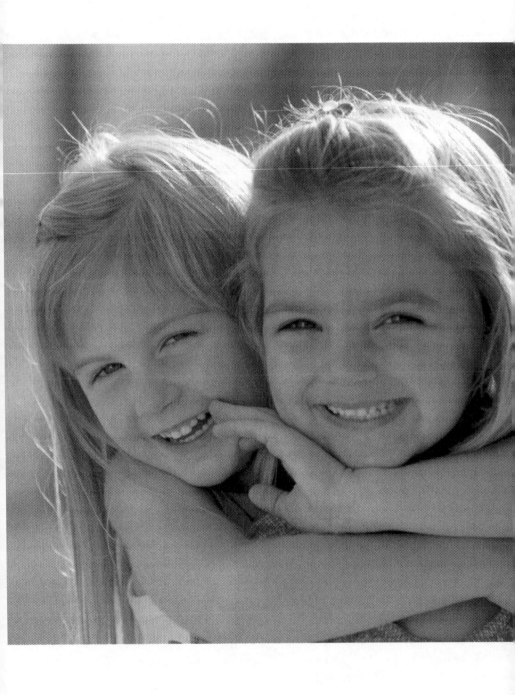

. . . because *Love* is a foretaste of *Heaven*.

My prayer for you is that
you know how wide,
how *long*, how *high*, and how *deep*
His love really is . . .
and that you *overflow*
more and more
with love for others.

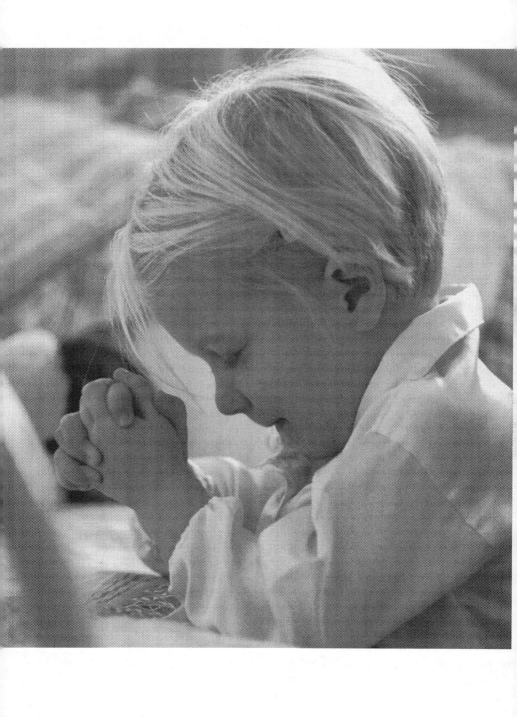

Notes

Page 12. *"Love is patient."* 1 Cor. 13:4.
Page 14. *"Love is kind."* Ibid.
Page 27. *"Love never fails."* 1 Cor. 13:8.
Page 31. *"I have loved you . . . "* Jer. 31:3.
Page 59. *"We love because . . . "* 1 John 4:19.

Do you have funny or heart-tugging pictures of your child? We would love to consider your photos for future inspirational baby books.

We need photos that are:
  • In digital format
  • At least 4 x 5 and 300 dpi

Submitting photos:
  • Please e-mail your photos to: photos@bordonbooks.com
  • In the subject line, put your last name.
  • It is helpful if you send one photo at a time.
  • Include your full name, address, and phone numbers with area code so we
    can contact you if your photo is accepted for publication.
  • If you would like, include a one-line caption for the photo.

When your photo is accepted:
  • We will ask you to sign a release for nonexclusive rights to publish your photo.
  • We will send you a complimentary copy of the book in which your child's
    photo appears. Additionally, we will credit you by name for the photo.

Thanks for your interest; we look forward to receiving your delightful photos.
Please e-mail your photos to: babyphotos@bordonbooks.com.

Printed in the United States
By Bookmasters